Dear Jon, Raechel, Jake, Duke + Daisy,

Thank you for taking good care of Nellie while we were on Martha's Vineyard! We know she'll miss you all. If you find yourselves missing her, we thought you might enjoy looking through this book. Debra Marlin is a Vineyard artist with a love for 'yellow dogs' ☺ ♥

With gratitude,
The Seidels

Lake's Soul

Lake's Soul

The Yellowdog Paintings

—————————◆—————————

Debra Marlin

Yellowdog Publishing

FIRST EDITION
FIRST PRINTING 2006
ISBN 978-0-9791077-1-9

BOOK DESIGN BY DEBRA MARLIN

For information on ordering other books by Debra Marlin, or limited edition prints: Giclées, or lithographs please visit www.yellowdoggallery.com or for information on purchasing the original paintings interpreted from the photographs in this book as well as related prints you may also visit www.lakessoul.com

Frontispiece: Photograph: Lake's Soul

I love you in a place where there's no space in time
I love you for my life you were a friend of mine,
and when my life is over remember that we were together
We were lone and I was singing a song for you.

– Leon Russell

The Eyes of a Dog

I have seen and lived in many places. From the lilting graceful shreds of Sun across the Lowcountry marshes of Charleston to the crashing prehensile waves of Big Sur I have seen the evidence of a Great Spirit in our world. I have appreciated gratefully the square cut of the most handsome jaw and been inspired by the gaze of the most feminine blue eyes in which again I saw proof of a Divine Plan. I have witnessed and known God in more things daily than I can write here but it is when I look into the eyes of a dog that I am most clear of my own task and gifts, and that I most feel the love that my Creator has intended for me. My spiritual instruction comes in that directive... to try, just try, to be and do what I see in those eyes.

"As his regal head rested in my palms and my thumbs stroked his soft muzzle
I gazed into his loving eyes and beheld a sweetness like no other
and I knew there was a God."

Debra Marlin

Trinity of Souls

The Intention

Yellowdog is to me the visual manifestation, the graphic translation of the knowledge that we exist in a field of vibrational frequency or subatomic particular motion. These vibratory speeds are determined on a holy quantum level by the degree of luminosity we exist in and project. It is my belief that the sounds, colors, and object forms we surround ourselves with, even on a seemingly mundane level, help determine our own level of particle movement. Essentially—there is magic in the air.

A force for inevitable change is blowing a clean clear wind through our consciousness. We as a species are evolving, being molded anew by the information in the vibrational field we choose to occupy. Color, shape, and tone are conveying information to us at a subconscious level. All stimuli have energy and all energy carries with it information. The greater the beauty and the truer that which touches our senses here in the material world is, the more accelerated the rate of vibration and ultimately the faster that information can be received, processed, and transmitted. Any image that is capable of evoking a feeling, eliciting a pure emotional response, is capable of producing love. These are the phenomena producing the highest vibrational rate and are the most transformative of the frequencies that can be accessed and implemented by man. Though an image may be a tree, a cloud, or a dog, there may be more than what is apparent. The shapes, shadows, and evocative power within an ostensibly perceived structure may in fact be an imperceptible bundle of information.

I wondered why I had always had such a need to "cast my eyes upon beauty." I now know why my spirit is enlivened by the sight of a dog. These paintings, which I have interpreted from the photographs of my dogs in the "Yellowdog" books, are an expression of the gratitude in my heart for the beauty and love of my dogs. Loving the dogs, photographing them and then painting their sweet faces has healed wounds from a hundred different lifetimes. My wish is that all who need solace will find it by falling into the eyes of the messengers that I have been so graced to know.

Tucker's Eyes

I told my dog Tucker today he was a really beautiful person. I laughed when I realized what I'd said but then affirmed to him that even though it was a slip of the tongue I meant it. Tonight I walked down the wide lantern lit street with him to our favorite coffee shop. As I sat and sipped, a bejeweled woman in a stole walked up and planted a kiss on his nose and told him he was a very elegant person. The next passerby commented on what a pure soul Tucker had. He gazed unblinking into every stranger's face who held his muzzle and told him of his beauty. He was the embodiment of peace as he held his presence still and lofty and received the truth of who he was while reflecting it back. Sometimes I am just a girl who loves her dogs but on this night I was the observer of all things important in the cosmos. I witnessed the simple absolution of worry in those fine people who were instantly returned to their own essences by the pure receptive love of a golden hearted dog. He looked fondly into their eyes and reminded them of their own perfect nature. After they had all passed I took his head in my hands and wondered what I might ever have done to be so blessed.

I had lost so much in the previous months and at times thought I lacked but tonight regarded myself as lucky and well provided for. I was rich in dog. The miracle that I could look into Tucker's eyes and be healed and reminded that there was still sense and love in the Universe was as great as any that could restore my fortune. As I photograph and paint the look that I see in Tucker's eyes I know that all is perfect in my world.

Lake's Soul

There are two kinds of dreams with which I am most familiar. There are those that come true and those that do not. I am fortunate in that most of mine have been simple enough to have a chance in the big world of aspiration. What I wanted from the time I can remember was to be an artist who lived by the sea with dogs and friends, a horse and a guitar. My dreams have all come true.

One winter's day as the Sun streamed into the room where I lie for my afternoon nap I saw it. While aromas from my mother's perfect Sunday meal wafted through the sunbeams in this moment of reverie I made my wish. Our dog lay in the cold dark garage which was his permanent station. Like every other day that I had begged that he be allowed to come in and nap with me "just this once," the answer was the same. Somewhere my childish petulant dismay turned from consternation to commitment. I decided that when I grew up my dogs would have the run of my life. And so they have. I am indeed a lucky girl.

It is a long journey they've taken with me. I have never been without them. I never saw them as God but rather as proof of the Mother/Father Protector and Creator. The fact that dogs exist is evidence enough for me. I have a painting that I did a while before my dog Lake died. It is called Lake's Soul. I painted it one day because I needed to feel and see the truth. It worked. The shortest route to what I sought was to look into the photograph in my hand and fall into the spiral of love that I saw in his eyes. I did just that and my large well worn paintbrush did the rest. As it swooped around the canvas I held it gingerly hoping with confidence that what I felt for my dog and he for me was enough to allow the piece to become. It was.

Lake, in his magnanimity had held still for longer than I deserved one Christmas Eve while we stayed in a cheap hotel room somewhere on a highway along our travels. As I adjusted the fake bronze lamp on the table next to the bed he patiently stared into my camera lens while I found the solace in his eyes I needed that night. I remembered what I received from him that cold lonely night as my brush continued its path and Lake lay at my feet.

The Veil

The secret of my life has been that I walk in a rhythmically pulsating bubble of light. In times of trouble I remember the first time I saw it. The day after I lost Lake I lay for a moment face up on my bed. Mustering up the energy to go into the day was for a moment more than I could bear. I was almost out the door when I had to turn around and try to collect myself. Powerless to fight back the tears that insisted on spilling out the sides of my eyes I lay there and surrendered to my heartache. The white ceiling above was a reminder of the words my mother had spoken to me as a child. When, at the age of four I asked her what the white swirling textured designs were she answered that it was God. She said that he was everywhere watching over and taking care of us. She said that God was in all things. I believed it then and I believe it now.

Suddenly I could see motion about a foot and a half above where I lay. A brilliant animation sprang to life and I could see a veil of white light turn to every color imaginable. It was a living thing. It was a glistening glassine veil from which the most beautiful light emanated. I knew at that moment that when I'd left the womb and the umbilical to the life blood from my mother had been cut it was just to that singular person who gave me entrance to the physical realm. I had never been separated from the divine source from whence I came and I surely would never be separated from that love. I couldn't see Lake in those moments of the benevolent reminder but I could feel his love. I have been aware many times since of the veil.

Long before I was consciously aware of the brilliant translucency we are enveloped in I made a decision to spend my life creating. Translating the appreciation I have at the abundance of beauty I see in the world thrills me. I am so better able to do it for the simple love of a dog.

Art is a fickle passion. Just as the muse will turn herself on again off again in her efforts to inspire, the fountain of abundance that flows most generously will flag at the times that call for a new dose of soul searching. I see it as the divine's gentle guidance and am grateful for it.

The Dog God

The slender girl with the long brown hair skipped gaily along the wooded path. The dappled afternoon light illuminated and warmed the verdant growth of the ancient way and turned the adjacent meadow of wildflowers to gold. She was flanked by two robins who flew playfully close to her head as a rabbit and deer kept pace. It was a gloriously beautiful day and she was happy for she had been summoned by the Dog God and was on her way to see him.

Late at night by the warm domed hearths her people would gather to share the stories they had heard of their home and its history. Legend told that this place was a magical kingdom that existed in all levels of time. It was a place that existed in the past, present and the future all at the same time. She had heard the stories and was fascinated but didn't think much about what others considered to be a conundrum, choosing instead to spend her time rolling down the steep soft pasture as the forest animals laughed in delight at her antics. Fun was the order of the day. The girl always listened more intently when a visitor spoke at one of the evening gatherings. The entire town grew animated when the visitors came by to share a dinner with them and tell what they knew of the Dog God. It was said that he resembled a great forest animal but that some who saw him thought he was not unlike themselves. Many told of meetings with him whereby they could hear his words but he could not be seen. More often than not the villagers spoke of having a sense of him but not hearing or seeing anything. All who ventured a tale spoke in a peaceful way as they carried their stories of the Dog God from town to town. The girl's favorite stories were the odes of journeying. There were a few visitors during the course of her life who told of being shown by the Dog God a place far away which was so like their own home. It was a place they had been sent to help care for and that somehow affected their own home. The young girl could not imagine leaving her beautiful home here for any reason. She would feel a great fear but also excitement when she heard of the far away place that the great being was known to send his bravest subjects.

As she frolicked through the grassy valley and up and down the hills toward the place she had been directed to go she knew she was far too young to have to worry about going anywhere. She knew only her own curiosity.

The morning of the girl's trek to see the Dog God was pleasant. She devoured her breakfast with gusto and retreated to the lawn behind her dwelling. Busying herself on the project she was building she interrupted her work intermittently to dance and tumble and lie in the grass looking up at the clouds. Each day was different for the children of her village. Every child was different so they were allowed their youth to play and create in whimsy. This morning as she lay contemplating her current task she could hear her parents in the house. The tone in their voices was serious as they spoke of the visitor of the previous evening. As the town folk had gathered for yet another evening of theatre and frivolity her parents had been summoned aside. They seemed a bit agitated as they made ready for slumber at evening's end and they were not very different this morning.

Her father came outside and interrupted the girl's sky watching. Putting his strong arm around her shoulder he pointed with the other toward the mountain at the edge of town. He told her that the visitor had informed him that she had been chosen to meet the Dog God. He spoke with grave concern while trying to comfort her. Giving her the lunch her mother had made for the hike he pondered the notion of his own child meeting the great being. Waving goodbye, the girl went on her way with relative ease. She had heard so many wonderful stories of others who had been called to climb the mountain. She felt safe for there was seldom cause for worry in the peaceful land that was their home.

The girl had been walking for about an hour. Traversing the path that wound up the hill she was joined by many animals. Anyone who knew the girl knew the delight she took in being with the forest creatures. They were fun to play with and she loved playing. Ascending the greatest incline she came upon a giant boulder that blocked much of the path. She squeezed between it and the side of the mountain. Walking a bit more she rounded the last curve and jumped back in astonishment. Beyond the mossy clearing at the top of the hill was a breathtaking vista. The brilliant blue of the afternoon sky seemed to meld into the dazzling sea that lay before her. She made her way around the remaining boulders and stood atop the grassy plateau surrounded by the blue enchantment. She stood transfixed as her right arm extended itself in a gesture that was a mixture of trust, affection, and supplication. There before her was the Dog God. He had a powerful though protective demeanor. The girl was awestruck. That thing in her chest that she had heard of referred to as Soul fluttered and suddenly grew very large. She struggled to regain her breath and when it came it was accompanied by a feeling of light air up and down her spine. Her entire body lifted and hung suspended a few feet off the ground.

His voice was soft but strong as he gestured toward her upward movement. "To repeat this you need only to feel about what it is you wish as you have just felt seeing me." She lifted a bit higher at the sound of his resonant tone. She had never felt so at ease and yet fully enlivened in her life. "Welcome, my child, I have been watching and know that you now must be shown the journey you were born to make."

The girl was transfixed by the beauty of the majestic deity and reveled in the glorious view she witnessed. Her blissful transcendence was interrupted as she found herself again standing firmly on the mountain plateau. The Dog God spoke. "I have called for you to come here so that I might instruct you on the ways of a place far in the distance but not so far from your heart. I know when you sleep you have dreamt of this place. It is a real place much like your home." He stood before her for a long time that seemed like moments. He answered so many questions she had lain awake at night pondering. The girl loved her life and wanted to make great use of her boundless energy. That afternoon she was shown what she must do.

"Look below you to the west," he motioned, "there is the place I am sending you." It will seem that you have left here forever but you will not really have traveled far. It is a place that you will go when you sleep. You must remember the lessons and instruction I give you now. You and many others like you will bring the spirit of our home with you and you will bring the beauty of the far away place back to us here. We will then be as one."

He continued. "This place you have come to today is like the place you are going. I know you do not understand but you are already there. When we part you will return home to your village and your family. When you sleep tonight you will go away to the new place. Do not worry. Time is not what you think it is and every morning when you wake you will rise in the home you have always known."

The girl stared at the beautiful blue green orb that had materialized before her. It was suspended in a mist of effervescent light and a lovely sound could be heard emanating from it. She took in the glory of the moment and agreed to all that the Master had requested of her. The thing he said that most filled her with joy was that she would be accompanied to the new place by many who were like him and looked as he did. She knew then that she could do almost anything.

Suddenly the sky darkened and the jovial countenance of the Great Dog changed as he turned to the horizon. His voice deepened and the girl stepped back as she listened. "The times you will know on your journey will not always be happy ones and the days may not all be the ones you'll want to remember. Life," he continued, "must have balance and in order for your time away to bear fruit and help us here, the times where your spirit will be tested are some of the most important. There will be joy," he paused drew a breath and looked lovingly at the girl, "but in order for it to exist there will be mighty storms that will take you quicker to your destination. Remember," he said as he moved closer dropping his head and softening his voice, "during the roughest seas you must lighten your grasp of the wheel and allow me to take over. This," he paused, "this will be the hardest thing you will have to do." The girl hastily agreed as she would say anything to get on with this new bold adventure. Knowing the courage and excess of gaiety in her heart he put his giant paw down firmly on her foot. "You won't remember most of what I am telling you until it is imperative that you are reminded. If you are lost or it is time for new direction I will always come to you in stillness with the command for you to remember and you will know the course to take. Listen closely to me now as you are a quick one and so eager. I am taking special care to keep you safe and you will have many guardians besides your animals to help you navigate. If you are quiet during the storms you will hear better their direction. I have given you and your kind a very special gift." He stopped for a moment to give the girl a chance to take in all that he said.

"As well as the animals and the beautiful places you'll live I will always send clear messages from my heart to yours. I am giving you something you will know on Earth as desire. Through those I have endowed with the power to speak with my voice I will send clear loving messages through your senses in the form of beauty and desire. This beauty comes from me but will be created by yourself and many like you. There will be glorious sound that your ears will hear, such as you cannot yet imagine. It will be accompanied by the ability many of you will have to put those sounds into shapes, colors, and form. You will always hear the messages I send and I will always soothe your spirit as you falter. Let your senses hear and see the work the creators do for me to help all who make this journey. The purpose of your time there is to create. When you do this you will answer the call of your most profound and sacred desires. It is then that you will know love, and love is your beautiful mission." The girl had settled down and was listening far more intently. She wanted to be one of the messengers to the senses.

The Dog God moved ever closer and the girl leaned into him to feel his warmth. She basked in the love and protection of the great and gentle beast. He began to move away from her and as a fog enveloped the blue green orb he spoke once more. "If you forget everything else I am telling you just remember one thing. Remember how powerful desire is and how it will bring love when you use it to create beauty. It will heal all things in all places in all time. This is your quest—to desire, to love and to create, leaving all else to me." He began to vanish as his last words lingered in the translucent afternoon haze. "If ever it is difficult to hear me or feel my love as you do now do this one thing. Look directly into the eyes of the friends I give you who look most like me and you will know me and know what you must do. You will know you are not lost... indeed I will be there with you. The animals and all the gifts I give you to fill your senses will guide you. If you do these things you will never be lost or alone."

The girl stared harder trying with her hands to part the fog that was fast enveloping the mountaintop. She rubbed her tear-filled eyes and began her descent to the valley below. Her greatest focus was on safely making it to the bottom before dark. By the time she arrived at the dirt road that would take her home she had forgotten much of her experience with the Dog God. He had said that she would.

That night at supper her father laughed musically and chided her for her profoundly colorful imagination. He had found her in a dreamy reverie earlier in the day. She was uttering faint musings about a beautiful beast and a far away blue green place. She had fallen asleep on the lawn while staring at the clouds.

Plates

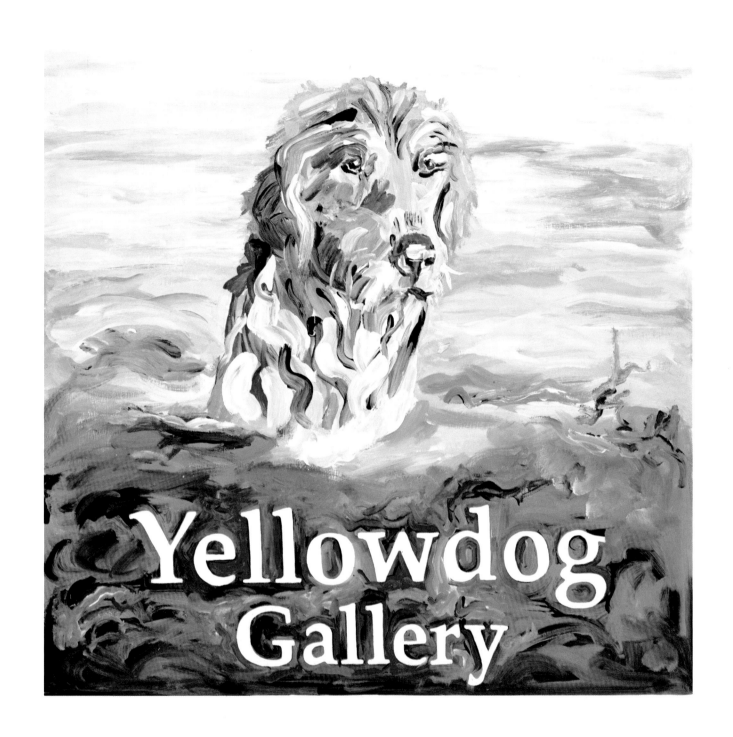

The Sign

Waterlove

Waterlove

Resurrection Waterlove

Waterlove III

Surf Fishing

Waterpup

Joy

Joy

A Deeper Shade of Joy

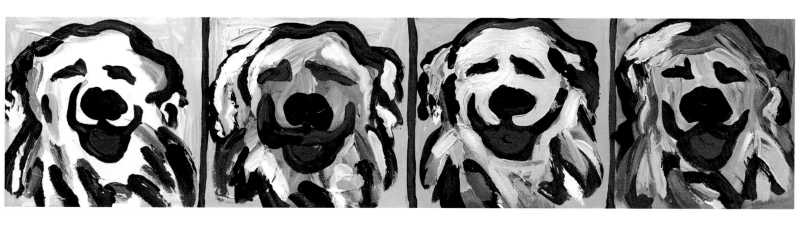

Winsome Joy

The Golden Laugh

Yellowdog

Summer Joy

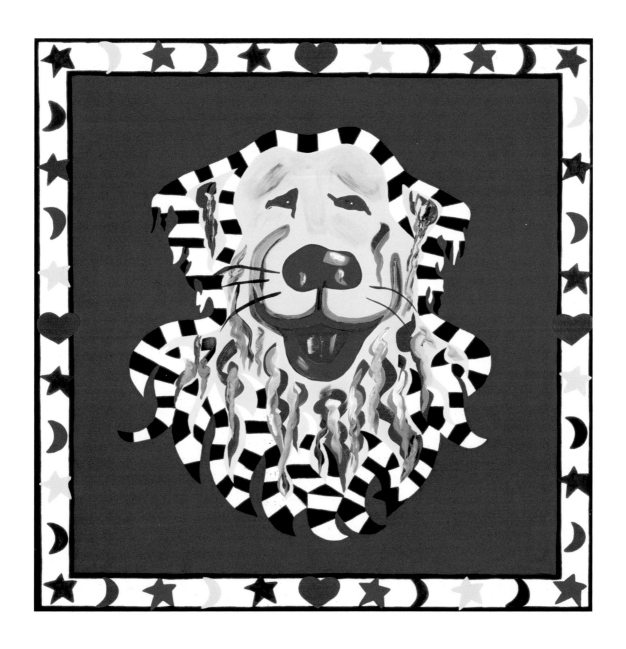

Ace of Dogs II

Light on Lake

Exponential Joy

Happy Dog

Ace of Dogs

Happiness

The Wild Ones

The Wild One

Truth

On Becoming a Wild One

Boone Dog

The Littlest Wild One

Wild One II

The Wildest One

River Emerging

The Wilder One

Lake's Soul

Lake's Soul

Lake's Beautiful Soul

Lake's Sweet Soul

Lake's Soul III

Transfiguration

Poignant Lake

Yellow Lake

Lake

The Many
Faces of Love

Morgan's Light

Little Ben

Buddy Boy

The Dog Boy

Breaker

The Dog Boy II

Sundog

Sweetheart

Portrait of a Puppy

Portrait of Breaker

The Incalculable Altitudes of Bliss

Sonny

Riverpup

Invitation

For most of her life the artist/author of the "Yellowdog" series, Debra Marlin, has been creating and producing jewelry, paintings, and photographs for her own exhibitions and galleries. In the last several years the interactive world of computers and the internet has made it possible for artists to showcase their work to a global audience and market with ever increasing immediacy. It is with great pleasure that you are now invited to enter the online galleries and view Debra's work at any time.

You are cordially invited to visit our web galleries where the work you have enjoyed in this and other books by this author are shown with the same elegant attention to detail that have been the hallmarks of her books and brick and mortar galleries. Debra has dedicated this time of great change and opportunity for all artists to creating books which she believes are the galleries of the future. These monographs are designed, along with the websites and soon to be created multi-media editions, to give the viewer the same personal experience that thousands have enjoyed in her actual galleries for years. A real time virtual gallery is now being created where it will be possible to visit the artist in her studio by appointment.

To order the images shown in this and Debra's newest work: "Yellowdog River of Love," please visit the web galleries or call 508-693-3466. "Yellowdog River of Love," and "Lake's Soul" are also available as elegant signed and numbered limited slipcover cased editions.

It is the author's fervent belief that this wonderful new digital realm is of enormous value when implemented by the artists and creators of the world. She pledges to continue to use this technology in all forms: music, film, still images and text so that admirers around the world may enjoy the work she is so proud of and grateful to create.

———————————————————————

Limited edition, signed and numbered, color lithographs of a selection of the images are available to order. We also offer a very limited edition of custom printed, signed and numbered Pigment Prints (Giclées). These stunning reproductions are printed on the highest quality, heaviest one hundred percent cotton archival watercolor paper. All Pigment Prints are presented in the size the originals were painted in. Original paintings are also available.

www.yellowdoggallery.com
www.lakessoul.com